The Seven C's of Positive Behaviour Management

Also in this series

Also by Sue Cowley

The Seven C's of Positive Behaviour Management

SUE COWLEY

Sue Cowley Books Ltd

2013

Sue Cowley Books Ltd
PO Box 1172
Bristol BS39 4ZJ
United Kingdom

www.suecowley.co.uk

© **Sue Cowley Books Ltd 2013**

First published in e-book format in 2012

All rights reserved. No part of this publication may be reproduced or transmitted in any form or by any means, electronic or mechanical, including photocopying, recording, or any information storage or retrieval system, without prior permission in writing from the publishers.

Sue Cowley has asserted her right under the Copyright, Designs and Patents Act, 1988, to be identified as Author of this work.

ISBN: 978-1489518200

Contents

Introduction

Welcome to this book, which offers you a tried and tested way to improve behaviour in your classroom. 'Positive Behaviour Management' is a set of practical approaches designed to help you get better behaviour from your students. The idea is that you get good behaviour in a proactive, forward thinking and creative way, rather than waiting for things to go wrong and having to pull back from a tricky position. All the ideas that I give in this book are based on my own experiences of what works with my students, on suggestions that other teachers have given me, on my experiences of training thousands of teachers in behaviour management, and on watching teachers at work in their classrooms. This guide is very much a practical, realistic and honest assessment of *what works* when it comes to managing behaviour.

The main philosophy behind Positive Behaviour Management is this: *I'm here to teach you, so I'm going to deal positively and proactively with anything that gets in the way of that goal, and that includes getting you to behave yourselves.* Or, to put it another way, imagine there's a sign over your classroom door, saying: *'This is how we do it here'**. Positive Behaviour Management is about creating an ethos where everyone works together to allow learning to happen. The ideas are straightforward to understand, and with persistence and hard work, they *will* make a difference to behaviour in your classroom.

In this book I deal with each of the ideas (the C's) in turn, giving an explanation of the key strategies and techniques involved, and why these work. You'll also find some suggestions for quick activities you can try yourself – *'TRY THIS'* – to develop your thinking and your learning further. If you're a parent as well as a teacher, you will find that many of the ideas are equally applicable to managing your own children's behaviour. Similarly, if you're not a teacher, but your job involves managing other people's behaviour, then again the ideas given here will work for you.

I'll keep this introduction short, because you'll want to get on to the 'meat' of the book – the ideas themselves. So, I'll finish by wishing you luck with managing behaviour, whether you're at the start of your teaching career, or someone experienced looking for fresh ideas or a new outlook. Remember, the best thing about managing behaviour better is that it means you can get on with the fun bit, which is, of course, the teaching.

Sue Cowley
www.suecowley.co.uk

* With many thanks to Paul Dix from Pivotal Education for permission to use his phrase.

Please note: I use the word 'students' throughout this book, to refer to the people you teach, whether they are children, teenagers, or adults.

The First C: Communication

High quality communication lies at the heart of good teaching, and of effective behaviour management. Teaching is about interaction between a teacher and his or her students. The more effective the teacher is at interacting – at communicating facts, information, attitudes, expectations, and so on – the more likely it is that the students will learn and behave. Or, to put it another way, if you want someone to behave in a particular way, *they have to actually understand what you're asking them to do in the first place.* This sounds easy to do, but it can be tricky to get right.

Five Steps to Success

Step One: Decide what behaviour you want from your students.

Step Two: Be realistic about how many things you can ask for at one time.

Step Three: Prioritise – don't expect to get everything in place all at once.

Step Four: Figure out how to phrase what you're asking for, so they really understand.

Step Five: Model what you've asked for, refer to it frequently and stick with it even when it's not easy.

Let's look at each of those steps in a bit more detail:

Step One: Decide what behaviour you want from your students ...

You've probably got a fair idea about the behaviour you want from your students. When you were studying to be a teacher, your lecturers would have called these your 'expectations'. The time it's hardest to figure this out is when you first become a teacher. I can remember getting to September of my *second* year, and thinking 'aha! *now* I know what I want from my classes'. Even if you're not 100% sure right now about what you want, it gets easier the more experienced you become. You can base most of it on your school or college rules, but you will have your own opinions and ideas as well.

Some of what you want to communicate will be the behaviours you *don't* want (mobile phones out, chewing gum, swearing); some will be the behaviours you *do* want (trying your hardest, bringing equipment).

TRY THIS: Make yourself a list of all the things you do and don't want from your students, in terms of their behaviour and also their attitude to learning. You could do this in two columns – a 'Do' column and a 'Don't' one.

Step Two: Be realistic about how many things you can ask for at one time ...

If I go into my classroom and reel off a list of twenty behaviours I want from my students, how many do you think they will actually retain? When I ask teachers this question, the optimists say 'three', the pessimists say 'one'. I suppose it depends whether your glass is half full or half empty ...

Some teachers get around this issue by working out a set of rules together with their students. The thinking is that this helps create a sense of community and partnership between the teacher and his or her class. As an approach it can be effective, so long as it fits with your style of teaching and you think it through ahead of time. However, it can also convey a sense of uncertainty to a class and the students may interpret it as a sign of weakness. Is this teacher telling them that she cannot decide these things for herself and expects the students to do it for her? My personal preference is to *tell* the students what I'm after – it saves time in the long run.

Which leads us neatly onto ...

Step Three: Prioritise – don't expect to get everything in place all at once ...

What you've got to figure out next is what you want to get in place first. Which of your key expectations are the *most* important to you? This will be different for every person reading this book – there is no one right or wrong way to do it. However, when I ask this question of teachers, some key ideas usually emerge every single time. The three key ideas that I often see are:

1. An expectation about how you want the students to listen.
2. An expectation about how you want the students to approach their learning.
3. An expectation about what the students should bring to class.

For instance, you might choose:

1. We listen in silence when someone is speaking.
2. We give it a go and work our hardest.
3. We arrive at lessons on time, and with the correct equipment.

Some teachers choose one key expectation to stamp on a class as their way of saying *this is how we do it here*. The expectation they choose might be a relatively minor behavioural issue, such as getting the students to do up their ties properly, or insisting that everyone stays in their seats. By having such a clear focus on a single expectation, the teacher communicates a message about his or her overall approach. Whether this would work for you is a matter of your personality, the type of setting where you work, and the kind of students you teach.

Once you've got those key expectations in place, and you're happy that the students are following them, you can introduce more expectations as you go along.

TRY THIS: Look at the list you made previously, about how you do and don't want your students to behave. Identify the three key expectations that you need to share with your class. Which ones are your priorities: those ones you see as vital to get in place first?

Step Four: Figure out how to phrase what you're asking for, so they really understand …

Now we're at the heart of the first 'C' – how to actually communicate to your students *what it is you want*. You'll have to find your own way to do this, but I can certainly give you some guidance as to what works best. Generally speaking, the best expectations are:

- ✓ Phrased in a positive way, i.e. do this, rather than don't do that;
- ✓ Short and crystal clear;
- ✓ About specific behaviours rather than generic ideas;
- ✓ Communicated in language that is appropriate for the age and background of the students;
- ✓ Something that everyone is going to do, with and for each other.

For instance, rather than saying: 'I don't want to hear any chatter or disrespectful behaviour when I'm trying to explain the lesson to the class', you could say 'I want complete silence when someone is talking' or 'We listen in silence to others', or even 'One person speaks at a time'. If you use the word 'we', you give the sense that this is the whole class and the teacher *working together*. The word 'I' can, however, give a greater sense of teacher control and clarity. It's up to you, and it's very much a matter of your own personal style and preferences.

Some teachers will use generic terms, such as respect or co-operation. There's nothing wrong with choosing to do things in this way. However, if you do use this approach, you've got to make sure there isn't a mismatch between what you *say* you want (e.g. respect) and how the students choose to *interpret* what you say you want (e.g. the 'street' version of the word respect). So, you will probably need to define with your class what these behaviours look like, or give them activities to do that show them how these words work in practice.

Step Five: Model what you've asked for, refer to it frequently and stick with it even when it's not easy …

Once you've communicated what you need to your students, you've got to help them get it in place. Their natural instinct will be to push at the boundaries; you've got to show them that doing what you've asked for is the best option all around. Used together, the Seven Cs will help you achieve this. In terms of the first C – Communication – you've got to reinforce your key expectations *through the way that YOU behave*.

Put it like this:

- ✓ If you *say* that you want them to listen to each other in silence, then you must … *never ever talk over them, or allow them to talk over each other.*
- ✓ If you *say* that we all work our hardest, then you must … *challenge them when they fail to live up to this, and work your hardest for them as well.*

As well as *showing* your students what these behaviours look like, you've also got to make the message stick in their brains. You can do this by referring to these behaviours frequently. This could include:

- ✓ Having posters on the wall, explaining your key expectations;
- ✓ Highlighting students who are giving you the behaviour you want;
- ✓ Incorporating rewards into your behaviour system, for instance praising a student who is behaving well.

And finally, you've got to stick at it, even when it's not easy (and most of the time it probably won't be). If, when times get hard, the students see you metaphorically throw your hands up in the air and say 'whatever', then they will believe that you have given up on them. No matter how hard it is, you need to stick with what you've asked for and, with time, your students will start to give you what you want.

The Second C:

Confidence

.

The Second C: Confidence

The irony is that, when you first become a teacher, confidence is the thing you most *need*, but also the thing you are least likely to *have*. The secret is to learn to pretend: to put on your 'teacher character' and become someone who looks and sounds confident, even if you're terrified inside. Because without a confident approach, the class will sense your weakness and hesitation, and prey on it. And without a sense of confidence and belief in what you are doing, you will over react to minor misbehaviour, rather than staying in control of the class and of yourself.

TRY THIS: Think back to when you were at school. Conjure up an image of two teachers who taught you – one who was confident and in control, the other who was nervous or aggressive or defensive. How did you and your class behave for each teacher and why?

The Confident Teacher

Confident teachers look like they mean what they say. This doesn't mean you should behave in an aggressive or pushy way – that's a recipe for disaster. You've got to learn to do it in a way that says (once again) *this is how we do it here*. Confidence is as much about perception as reality – about the way that your students 'read' you, usually within the first few minutes of meeting you.

Let me emphasise, you don't have to *feel* confident in order to mimic the attributes of a confident person. Incorporate some or all of the following techniques, and you will magically appear more confident:

✓ Move freely around your room or teaching space, visiting every part of the room to mark it as your own.

- ✓ Have some moments of stillness as well, to hint at your deep inner reserves of self belief and self confidence.
- ✓ Make plenty of eye contact – 'machine gun' the class with your eyes, so that you create the sense of a bond between you and your students.
- ✓ Move in towards a student when he/she answers your questions, to show interest and encourage others to respond.
- ✓ Maintain an upright posture, breathing calmly and holding your head up high, especially when things are going wrong.
- ✓ Use a clear voice, with no pauses or fluffs, but with plenty of tone, interest and variety.
- ✓ Maintain a sense of pace: in your speech, in your teaching, and in your lessons.
- ✓ Be enthusiastic and passionate about the job that you do. If you truly believe that teaching is a valuable and vital occupation, this will shine through to your students.
- ✓ Smile, to show your students that you like them.

There are many different types of confidence. Some teachers use a dramatic approach, where confidence is expressed through an outgoing and extroverted attitude. Other teachers use a quietly confident style, and come across as having a powerful inner sense of self belief and self esteem. Still others use a business like attitude, where confidence is expressed through clarity and efficiency. Each of these approaches will help you manage behaviour more effectively. Find the confident teacher persona that most closely matches your own personality, so that you can maintain it in the long term.

The Confident Lesson

As well as looking confident, you also need your teaching to convey a sense of confidence. You need your lessons, and the way they are taught, to come across in a confident manner. You need them to feel well organised, to have a sense of flow and forward motion, to be interesting, engaging and well managed. To show you what I mean, let's think about this in a business context, rather than a teaching one.

Imagine this: you arrive at an important meeting and the director of the company, who is meant to be running the meeting, isn't there yet. When she does arrive, she flaps around, looking hot and flustered, and she doesn't have the correct papers with her. She tries to get a projector going to show some figures, but it doesn't work. Then, she spends the whole meeting droning on about what has gone wrong in past meetings, and how you're all heading for disaster.

How would you feel after that meeting? How successful do you think her business would be? And how might you behave at the time, and in the future, for this person? Now, if you transpose this to a teaching setting, you can see why it's so vital to project a sense of confidence through your lesson preparation.

To create a confident feeling lesson:

✓ Be crystal clear ahead of time about what your lesson involves – what it's going to help the students to learn, and also how it will be organised.
✓ Communicate this information to your students when they arrive, so that they feel that you're well organised and in control of the situation. Make them believe that they're going to learn something useful in your lesson.

✓ Have all the resources you need ready, to hand, having checked that they are *all working* (especially anything that involves technology). Make sure you have enough of everything and, if you don't, figure out how you're going to share the resources you do have amongst the students.

✓ Give a sense of pace and momentum to your lesson, through the way you introduce the activities, through the speed of your voice and through your non verbal gestures.

✓ Encourage the students to believe that they are learning something new, interesting or valuable by making it *sound* new, interesting or valuable (even if it's not).

✓ Give the students at least some element of choice and input into the way that the lesson progresses.

TRY THIS: If you struggle with getting your lessons flowing smoothly, run them through in your head, like a movie, before they happen. You can even say the words you plan to use out loud, so you get your 'script' really clear in your mind. The clearer you are, the more confident you will appear.

The Confident Classroom

Your classroom (or other teaching space) is your domain, your kingdom if you will. That is, unless you are forced to move from room to room to teach – my commiserations if this applies to you. With your own teaching space, you can convey a sense of confidence simply through how your room *looks* when your students arrive. They will make snap judgements when they arrive at your room, particularly in the first few times they are taught by you. Your aim should be to build an atmosphere where *you* appear to be fully in control.

15

To create a confident looking classroom:

✓ Have a code of conduct or a set of rules, sanctions and rewards displayed on your wall, where you can refer to it. Make this as large as feasible, so that it's easily visible to the students. Indeed, there's nothing wrong with making it huge – this will certainly grab your students' attention.
✓ Avoid too much clutter – no piles of papers or unmarked books lying around the room (hide them in a cupboard if necessary). Make sure your students can focus on any important visual messages that are on the walls, and also on you and your teaching.
✓ Think about how you lay out your room, and consider how room layout impacts on your students' behaviour. If you're really struggling with behaviour, change your room around to shock/surprise your students into rethinking their approach.
✓ Just generally keep your room neat and tidy – for instance, putting folders into a neat pile and wiping your whiteboard between lessons.

TRY THIS: Take a walk around your school or college after the working day has finished. Have a peak in other people's teaching spaces, and ask yourself whether their rooms have a confident atmosphere or not. If they do, what is special about them? If they don't, why is this?

The Third C:

Carrots and Consequences

The Third C: Carrots and Consequences

The third C is a double C – the carrots and consequences that you use to motivate your students to do as you ask. Motivation is a very complex beast, with different people being motivated by very different things. You will need to make use of both carrots (rewards) and consequences (sanctions) in order to control your students' behaviour.

TRY THIS: Think for a few minutes about why it is that you turn up for work every morning. Yes, it will be at least partly about your salary, because you need to put food on your table and pay your mortgage/rent. But why specifically did you become a teacher? What is it about being a teacher that truly motivates you? Why did you choose this profession over all the others you could have chosen?

Making the Most of Carrots

Most of us respond far better to the carrot than the stick. We'd rather be persuaded to do something through positive methods, than forced to do something through fear of what will happen if we don't. For this reason, always use carrots first, before moving on to use consequences if they really are needed. Use many more carrots than consequences, and remember that rewards do not have to be 'things'. A smile or a word of praise from a teacher the students admire is rewarding in its own right.

Some students have a high level of self motivation (sometimes called 'intrinsic' motivation). These students are generally from supportive homes, where the adults place a value on education, and where there's a sense of interest in and curiosity about learning. Other students need far more external input (or 'extrinsic' motivation), because they find it so hard to motivate themselves. These students are often from a difficult background, and are typically the ones who struggle to behave. You may find yourself handing out far more carrots to this latter group of students, because they need that constant drip feed of motivators.

When they are young, children are generally fairly easy to motivate, mostly because they really want to please *you*. Your carrots will sound exciting to them, even if it's something as simple as a sticker, a certificate or a lucky dip. As students get older, they become ever more world wise and cynical. Consequently, you need to think creatively about how you can make your rewards as appealing as possible. One great idea is to ask *them* what rewards they would like to receive.

Many school systems rely on motivators that are hopelessly out of touch with what the students truly want. So, what teachers often do is create their own reward system to run alongside the official one. This alternative system may run relatively close to the edge in terms of what is allowed, for instance the teacher might play the students music if they work well, or give them treats, such as sweets or time on the internet.

To motivate your students:

✓ Use the school or college system of rewards consistently, whenever you can;
✓ Give lots of verbal praise and non verbal signals (a smile);
✓ Develop your own system of rewards, one that works for your students;
✓ Make a point of rewarding effort, as well as attainment;
✓ Be fairly hard to please, rather than someone who gives rewards easily;

✓ Make the learning really exciting, something they truly *want* to do.

For a free downloadable list of useful rewards and sanctions, visit my website www.suecowley.co.uk.

Making the Most of Consequences

Just as with carrots, you've got to get consequences right to manage behaviour effectively. For each behaviour you don't want, there needs to be a specific consequence that you will apply if that misbehaviour happens. In this way, you can train your students not to present you with these behaviours in class. However, that's not to say that you spot a misbehaviour, slap on a consequence and things will magically be okay. As with most things involving human beings, it's an awful lot more complicated than that.

Before you apply the more formalised consequences, such as a detention or a phone call to the student's home, use lots of low key and non verbal signals. These become unspoken cues that tell the student that you're not happy. You might:

✓ Look over at the student, and raise an eyebrow;
✓ Clear your throat or make some other noise;
✓ Move over to the student and stand beside him or her;
✓ Highlight a student who is already behaving as you wish.

It's also important to consider what *caused* the problem behaviour in the first place. Is this student's behaviour telling you something about your lesson? Has the pace slumped, or is the learning too difficult? Or is the behaviour telling you something about the student? Is he struggling to keep up? Does she have a very short attention span? This is not to say that you should automatically assume problem behaviour is your fault. However, you should consider what the causes are so that you can adapt your approaches accordingly.

A very useful way of understanding how people behave around consequences is to consider your own responses to them as an adult, and specifically if you drive a car. In the United Kingdom, the speed limit on motorways is 70 miles an hour. But these days, who sticks to that limit? We've all been pushing at the boundaries for so long, it is as though we've magically moved them, all by ourselves.

Imagine this scenario, to think about how your behaviour changes according to the kind of consequences you are likely to receive:

✓ You're driving along the motorway – what speed are you going?
✓ All of a sudden, up ahead of you, you spot a police car.
✓ What happens to your behaviour and why?
✓ Once the police car is out of sight, what happens to your speed?
✓ Now imagine that it starts to pour heavily with rain – does your behaviour change?
✓ Why do you behave differently in this particular situation?
✓ Eventually you come off the motorway, drive into a residential area and past a school. It's the end of the day at the local school, and there are children spilling into the road.
✓ What happens to your behaviour in this particular scenario and why?

Thinking about your responses to that scenario should help you understand how to make consequences work well for you. To be effective, consequences need to:

✓ Be seen to be applied and followed through on;
✓ Be something that the students really want to avoid;
✓ Include a visual element and a feeling of authority (the police officer's uniform);
✓ Be closely linked to your students' own personal safety or well being;
✓ Be about a moral duty that they owe to others.

This final notion – that we should behave well because we owe it to others – is perhaps the strongest motivator of all for changing people's behaviour. If you can encourage your students to see how their behaviour impacts on *others*, and particularly on their peer group, they are far more likely to make the changes you want to see.

TRY THIS: Have a long, hard think about the consequences that actually work with your most difficult students. Often, the typical school or college sanctions will barely touch a very troubled student, because he or she will have experienced far worse in life already. What can you use as a consequence that will really mean something to these students? That's not to say that you should work out the toughest, meanest, nastiest punishment you can possibly give. Rather, that you might need to think more creatively when dealing with this kind of student.

The Fourth C:

Consistency

The Fourth C: Consistency

Consistency is about clarity, about fairness, and about treating your students in the right way. It's about letting your students know, ahead of time, what the rules are, and what will happen if they refuse to comply with these rules. Then, it's about sticking to what you said – about being true to your word. Put simply, consistency means that if you tell your students behaviour 'a' will lead to consequence 'b', then that is what must happen every time. When you achieve this, your students soon learn that they must avoid certain behaviours, to avoid certain consequences. They also learn that you are trustworthy – that you mean what you say.

To make consequences work consistently:

✓ The same behaviour must receive the same teacher response, every time it happens.
✓ The students must know about the consequences of their behaviour ahead of time, rather than this being something that you throw at them without any warning.
✓ The consequences must be something that they definitely want to avoid. If they don't see these as enough of a punishment, they won't care if you apply them.
✓ You've got to follow through on what you've said you're going to do, every single time. This will be hard when you are stressed, tired or busy.

The more you follow through, the better behaviour you will get, because your students will see that you mean business. Remember, it shouldn't matter whether this is the first time a student has shown you this particular misbehaviour, or the fiftieth: the response should be exactly the same. In other words: *This is how we do it here.*

Why Consistency Matters

Consistency matters: for you, for your students, and also for the other staff at your school or college. If you understand *why* it's important, you should find it easier to maintain the effort required to achieve it, even when you're feeling tired and over worked. Consistency matters because:

- ✓ The students know exactly what to expect when they come to your lessons. If you constantly present them with different teacher personas, they may get thrown or become upset.
- ✓ It helps you create patterns and routines for the way that your lessons run. These in turn give the students a feeling of safety and security, which they may well be missing at home.
- ✓ Eventually your life becomes easier, as your students see that you are always going to follow through. They learn to stick to the rules because they want to avoid those consequences.
- ✓ Staff are seen as a team, working together towards a common goal and supporting each other. The ethos becomes one of positive cooperation between all the members of the institution.
- ✓ The students cannot play off staff, one against another, by saying 'so and so lets us do that, why won't you?'
- ✓ It's only fair, really, to apply the same rules in the same way to everyone.

Types of Consistency

There are two basic types of consistency: cross school consistency, where all staff aim to apply the same rules and consequences to every student, and individual consistency, where the teacher treats all of his or her students in the same way. It is very frustrating when you feel you are applying the rules, and following through on the consequences, but hardly anyone else seems to be bothering. Unless you are a member of senior management, you may not be able to persuade other staff to follow the approach you're using. However, that certainly doesn't mean you should give up, no matter how tempting it becomes to do so. As the saying goes, be part of the solution, rather than part of the problem.

You should also consider very carefully how consistently you treat individual students within your own class or classes. Often, teachers will react differently to a student who constantly misbehaves, because they are so fed up with the student refusing to change his behaviour. It starts to feel personal, you get into frequent arguments, and the student begins to feel that you don't actually like him.

TRY THIS: Think of a student you teach, one who really gets on your nerves. Then think of another student, one who you feel is absolutely lovely. Now imagine a situation in which both of these students are misbehaving in exactly the same way. Be honest —would you react in exactly the same way to both of them? Or would you react more negatively to the student who always irritates you?

Where the teacher is inconsistent in his or her handling of individual students:

* ✗ It reinforces the negative aspects of the relationship;
* ✗ The student will claim the teacher is 'picking on him';
* ✗ The teacher begins to believe that the student holds a grudge;
* ✗ The teacher highlights every little thing the student does wrong;

✗ There's a sense of injustice and inequality;

✗ The student may act up in front of his peers, to try and regain status.

As a professional, you must try your very hardest not to allow your personal emotions about your students to influence the way you treat them – either for good or for bad.

Flexible Consistency

The issue with a completely consistent and unbending approach is that it doesn't take into account the infinite variety of human reactions and responses. In every teaching situation, there will be some instances where a flexible approach to consistency is required. This is not to say that the *standards* are flexible, it's just that you need to use flexibility in the way that you *go about getting* those standards. You're after the same end result – behaviour 'a' – from different students. It stands to reason that you may need to use different approaches to get that same result.

For instance, imagine you teach two very different students. Child 'a' is a very gentle, well behaved and intelligent child, who usually behaves impeccably in your lessons. Child 'b' has been violent towards staff in the past, often behaves in an appalling manner, and really struggles with the learning. One day in class, you notice that *both* these students are not doing their work. Here's where flexible consistency comes into play …

With child 'a', you might give a short, sharp, focused command, such as 'I need you to get on with your work right now, thanks.' The child will most likely apologise and get back onto task straight away. But with child 'b', you might decide to go and have a one to one chat about what's going on. Using a relaxed tone and low key body language, you check whether he needs any help with the work and let him know what rewards he will receive if he manages to finish a certain amount of the work.

The end result is the same – you've explained to both students that they need to get on with their work. However, the approaches you've used are very different, because of your professional understanding of these children and your ability to be flexible. As is often the case in teaching, a very useful motto to have is 'whatever works'.

The Fifth C: Control

In any class, someone has got to be in control, and ideally you want it to be you. Because if you're not in control, then one or more of your students will be. And the ones who will most likely take control are those who wish to disrupt your lessons and prevent any learning taking place (they're kids so they would call it 'boring hard work' rather than 'learning'). Interestingly, as well as *you* wanting it to be you who is in control, most of your *students* also want it to be you that is in control.

It's not your job as a teacher to create some kind of democracy, where everyone has an equal say in how things should be run. Whilst in theory this might be a lovely notion, it's just not realistic and not very much learning would take place. Rather, you need to achieve a form of benign dictatorship, where you control most of what happens, but your students feel that you respect them, and allow them to have their say from time to time.

That's not to say that you have to be some kind of control freak, who is rigid about behaviour and who refuses to let the students have any input into their lessons. Remember: all this behaviour management stuff you're doing has *one purpose,* and *one purpose only.* And that is to allow teaching and learning to take place in your classroom. With perhaps thirty students in a room, not everyone can have their way or their say at all times. Don't feel guilty about taking charge: you're doing it for the benefit of the students, to make sure that they can learn.

TRY THIS: Think back to when you were a school child. Do you remember a teacher who couldn't control the class? What did it feel like being in his or her lessons? What was it about this teacher that meant the students could take control? What lessons can you learn from those memories to inform your own teaching?

Control Yourself

When it comes to controlling a class of students, the first thing you must control is yourself. You've got to learn to stay calm, even when a student/class is behaving really badly. Most teachers will lose their tempers and shout at some point, but in the long run the key to success is getting your own reactions and emotions under control. Because if you don't, the students will look at you and realise how easy it is to wind you up. And this will give them an incentive to mess you around again in the future.

It's very tempting to react instantly to every example of poor behaviour, but your initial, emotional response will often not be the most effective one. Unless the misbehaviour is very serious or dangerous, the world is not going to end if you don't deal with it the very instant it happens. Instead, try this:

✓ Notice the misbehaviour, but make a deliberate decision not to react to it. Look away and check what is happening elsewhere in the classroom.
✓ Take some deep breaths, and then perhaps give a 'look' to the student to see if that will be enough to stop the misbehaviour.
✓ If not, say something like 'I'll come and speak to you in a moment' and again refocus your attention on the rest of the class.
✓ At this point, you might praise a positive behaviour from a student who is behaving exactly as you wish.
✓ Set a task that the class can do for a few minutes, without needing any teacher input.

✓ When the rest of the students are focused and on task, move over to the misbehaving student.

✓ Crouch down beside him or her, and outline the 'choice' that he or she must make (see the following section – the Sixth C).

✓ Now walk away. A few minutes later, if necessary, come back to see what decision the student has made. .

✓ If the student has made the wrong decision, reinforce the choice again or apply the consequence.

✓ Alternatively you may find that the student has adapted his or her behaviour, and that you don't need to intervene again.

As well as controlling your temper, and the way that you handle individuals, you can also control how you come across visually. Your choice of clothing, and all the other visual aspects of your appearance, will have an impact on how your students behave for you. If you want to be viewed as business like and efficient, then wear a suit. If you'd like to be viewed as the crazy creative, then wear colourful, eccentric clothing. If you turn up looking sloppy and unkempt, then don't be surprised if this is how your students perceive your teaching style as well.

Control Your Voice and Your Body

The way that you use your voice and your body will have a profound effect on the kind of behaviour you get from your students. What you want is for your students to perceive you as calm, relaxed, in control and able to engage with and inspire them. All this (and much more) will come across in the way that you speak to your students, and the signals that you send with your body. However, you can also send some very negative messages with your voice and your body, often without even realising you are even doing it.

Let's look first at the negatives – those approaches you want to avoid. These are the verbal and non verbal signals that suggest stress, defensiveness, nerves or loss of control. When it comes to the way you speak, these include:

- ✖ A high pitched voice;
- ✖ Or, a voice that gradually goes higher and higher in pitch;
- ✖ Speaking very fast and becoming breathless;
- ✖ Talking in a hesitant or very slow manner;
- ✖ Making lots of mistakes within your speech;
- ✖ Giving overly long or rambling explanations;
- ✖ Excessive use of technical vocabulary;
- ✖ Lots of 'umms' and 'errs';
- ✖ A lack of tone and interest in the voice.

And when it comes to the way that you use your body, you need to avoid:

- ✖ Standing with your arms crossed all the time;
- ✖ Backing yourself up against the wall;
- ✖ Slumping over;
- ✖ Biting your lip, or chewing a finger;
- ✖ Constantly moving around the room in a nervous manner;
- ✖ And also, not moving at all.

Now let's think about the positive signals, those ones you *want* to send. The way you talk needs to:

- ✓ Be relaxed, with a conversational level of pitch;
- ✓ Feel lively, with a good pace, although not too fast;

✓ Sound clear, with precise diction, so that each word can be heard;

✓ Be concise, using vocabulary at an age appropriate level;

✓ Put emphasis on key words, so that the students can pick them out and retain them;

✓ Be full of tone and interest, again as appropriate to the age of your students.

And your body needs to:

✓ Be held upright, with your head erect on your shoulders;

✓ Look relaxed, with shoulders down and arms unfolded;

✓ Have a sense of flow and movement around the room;

✓ Include moments of stillness when you refocus and engage with the class.

Control Your Students

As well as controlling yourself, you should also think carefully about how you can control your students. This is not to say that you want to turn them into robots, controlled and manipulated by their teacher. However, by controlling what they do at certain points in a lesson, behaviour will improve. You will be freed up to get on with teaching, and they will be freed up to get on with learning.

There are several different times within a lesson where you might wish to control the students:

✓ **The way that they enter the room:** Wherever possible or appropriate, ask your students to line up before you invite them into your room. This allows you to control their entry, checking uniform if they wear it, making positive comments, or simply saying 'good morning' to them.

✓ **The way that you organise seating:** By having a seating plan, you create a sense that you are in control of the class, and that there is a certain formality in your approach. You also ensure that you don't get friends sitting next to friends, which often results in more chatting than working.

✓ **The way that they move around the room, or between tasks:** Control these times, for instance by allowing one table of students to move at a time. You might also use a time signal, such as a count down, to give them the motivation to change around quickly.

Control Your Classroom

The way that you manage your classroom or other teaching space will have a powerful impact on your students' behaviour within that space. From the moment they first meet you, your students will be making judgements about you based on what they see of your room. Whether these judgements are correct, fair or appropriate is not really the point. You've got to deal with the reality of the situation.

TRY THIS: Step outside your classroom and then walk into it with completely fresh eyes, as though you had never seen it before. What do you notice first? What are the positives about this space? And what negatives can you spot? If you were a student, what would you say or think about the kind of teacher who works within this space?

The way that you set out the desks or tables within your room will impact on behaviour, and also on the students' perceptions of how they should behave. Think about the approaches you want to use, and the signals you'd like to send:

✓ Where desks are set out in rows, students will generally perceive the teacher as being a bit old fashioned, and having a formal approach.
✓ Where desks are set out so students can sit in groups, they will tend to perceive the teacher as taking a more relaxed and group based approach to learning.
✓ Where desks are put in a 'U' shape, the students may view the class as more of a collaborative learning situation, where everyone is encouraged to contribute.

Control Your Lesson

The way that you pace and time your lesson will also have a direct impact on the way that your students behave during the class. If the atmosphere in the lesson starts to drag, then the students will probably begin to mess around, to keep themselves awake. Similarly, if the speed of the lesson is too fast, the students may disengage because they cannot keep up with what the teacher is telling them.

To get the best behaviour during your lesson:

✓ Be aware of how your students look – are they engrossed, are they zoning out, are they starting to fidget?
✓ Don't stick rigidly to a lesson plan, especially if it's not working. Be flexible enough to think on your feet and adapt your lesson content or timing as required.
✓ Talk to your class frequently about time. Let them know how much of it they have left to complete a task, how much they have used already, how well they are doing in relation to time targets, and so on.
✓ Control the way you handle resources within the lesson. Use the chance to give out resources as a reward for good behaviour. Consider bringing volunteers to the

front of the class to demonstrate the use of resources, before you hand them out to the rest of the students.

✓ Control the end of your lesson, making sure your students leave in a calm and ordered frame of mind. This will influence how they behave the next time that they see you, because this time in the lesson will be uppermost in their memories.

The Sixth C:

Choice

The Sixth C: Choice

As human beings we are constantly making choices about our behaviour – choices that impact on our lives in both positive and negative ways. Our students are a bit less experienced than us in making the right choices, so we need to help them learn how to do it properly. When it comes to behaviour, some of the choices we make are really vital ones, with the potential to do great harm or great good in our lives, and the lives of others. Should I steal that car/hit that person/throw a brick through that window? Should I study for that qualification/write that book/help that friend who's in trouble?

Help your students understand that there is a link between the choices they make about how to behave, and the consequences that follow those decisions. This will help them a great deal with their behaviour, both in your classroom and also in their lives beyond the school gates. You are, essentially, preparing them for their grown up, adult lives – holding down a job, having a family, doing well in the world.

The Language of Choice

The ideal situation is for your students to understand that *their* behaviour is *their* choice. Yes, there will be external influences on their behaviour, but no one can force them to do good, or indeed bad, things. The decision is theirs to make. Yes, some young people are dragged into terrible behaviour by their peer group, but others have the strength of character to resist. You want your students to find the strength to say: 'no, I'm not doing that'.

In any case, you are not there to force them to behave, you are there to teach them, and to help them all to learn.

The reason you have to manage their behaviour is so that you can allow learning to take place in your classroom. Don't feel bad about handing over the choices to your students. The realisation that *you* can decide how you choose to behave is a key step in taking responsibility for your own life.

You can use a kind of 'script' to help your students understand this concept. In your script, you outline what a good choice might look like, and equally what will happen if they choose to do the wrong thing. Your script might look something like this:

'Andrew, you have a choice. You can do the work now, and perhaps even earn yourself a reward. Unfortunately if you refuse to do the work during lesson time, I will be forced to keep you in at break time to finish it. And I really don't want to do that.'

Or this …

'Amelia, you have a choice. You can sit down in your seat now, and stay there for the rest of the lesson. That way we'll get along just fine. Unfortunately, if you choose to get out of your seat again, and disrupt my lesson, I'm going to be forced to give you a verbal warning. And that's something I'd really prefer not to do.'

Often, when you outline the choices in this way, a student will try to argue back, saying 'it's not fair' or 'why should I have to do that?'. Where this happens, teachers will often get sucked into a debate, but really there is no need. Why dignify the argument with a response? Ignore the student's complaints, repeat what you have said and, if the student insists on making the wrong choice, follow through on the consequences you have outlined.

As a very wise head teacher once said to me: *Be reasonable, but don't reason with them.'* In other words, you're the adult and you get to decide what is and is not acceptable in your classroom.

Choices about the Learning

You can also introduce an element of choice into your students' learning. This should have a beneficial impact on their behaviour, because it helps them feel that you trust and believe in them. They will see that you are giving them responsibility for making good choices in all areas, not just about their behaviour.

To do this, you might:

- ✓ Offer them two or more different ways of approaching an activity and allow them to choose the one they prefer;
- ✓ Ask them to devise a list of questions that they would like answered, on a topic that you need to cover;
- ✓ Encourage them to participate in teaching the lesson, so that they can have an influence on how their peer group learns.

The Seventh C: Creativity

Teaching is very much a creative activity, one that is full of opportunities for lateral thinking and imaginative approaches. It's my firm belief that you do yourself and your students a disservice if you don't view your role in this way. You can incorporate creative approaches when you're planning a lesson, and equally you can use creative ideas when you're managing behaviour. Both forms of creativity will enhance the day to day experience in the classroom, both for you as the teacher and also for your students.

Of course, there are many things that can mitigate against you being as creative as you might like. You might be put under pressure to achieve certain results, you could be due for an inspection. You may worry about what others will say, or you could lack the experience needed to be experimental. My advice is to start small, perhaps with a single activity, and develop from there.

Ask yourself, at every opportunity: 'How can I get the best behaviour and learning from my class?'. Learn to trust your own judgement as a highly trained professional. Don't simply accept other people's opinions about what you 'should be doing' – question them if you don't feel they are valid. In teaching, opinions about the best way to teach or to manage behaviour are changing and developing all the time. You need to have faith in your own philosophies and beliefs. This is all part of developing a confident teacher persona.

Thinking Laterally about Behaviour

There are three main ways to get people to behave differently: you can motivate or reward them to do as you wish; you can sanction them if they refuse to do what you want; or you can try something completely different. When you come across a behaviour problem that you can't solve, despite trying the classic strategies, think laterally about what else you might try. If the traditional techniques aren't working, then aim to come up with something new, fresh, different, weird, unusual, funny, odd, mad, whatever. It's probably easiest to understand this if I give you some real life examples from my own and other people's teaching.

For instance, if my students constantly forget to bring a pen to lessons I could ...

✓ **Reward them:** Give a sticker, a merit, a praise postcard to those who do bring a pen.
✓ **Sanction them:** Have a clear consequence, e.g. a break time detention, for those who don't bring a pen.
✓ **Get creative:** Tell them they can borrow a pen, but it's 'a pen for a shoe', i.e. they have to give me one of their shoes in return for me giving them a pen. Hopefully this should be sufficient to embarrass them into bring a pen next time around.
✓ **Get creative:** Have a pot of pens available to give to my students, but with a 'fine' each time they use one. The class can nominate a charity of their choice to receive the money.

Similarly, if my students constantly get out of their seats during lessons I could ...

✓ **Reward them:** Note and praise those who stay in their seats throughout the lesson, and let them leave first at break time.
✓ **Sanction them:** Have a definite sanction for getting out of their seats, for instance a verbal/written warning or a yellow/red card system.

45

✓ **Get creative:** Tell them that if I happen to notice that they are out of their seats, I'll just have to assume that they don't actually *want* a seat, and I will remove it for a period of time.

✓ **Get creative:** Think about whether the class needs a more active approach and, every ten minutes, get them all up and doing some movement exercises. Anyone who gets out of their seat before this time has to 'freeze' like a statue while the rest of the class does the exercises. This should hopefully encourage them to channel all that energy in a more positive way.

Whether you can use these more creative approaches will depend on your relationship with the class. When they don't know you very well, attempts at humour can sometimes come across as sarcasm. Start by using the more traditional style of rewards and sanctions and then, once you get to know the students a bit better, incorporate some of these more unusual ideas.

Teaching and Learning and Behaviour

There's a very intimate link between the quality of teaching and learning you provide for your students, and the kind of behaviour you're going to get from them in return. That's not to say that it is your *fault* that your students misbehave, because your lessons are rubbish. Equally it is not to say that behaviour will suddenly and magically improve just because your lessons get more interesting. However, I do believe it's fair to say that you are *more likely* to get good behaviour from a class of students if they are engaged and they see the learning as being relevant and of value to them as individuals. At the very least, they may forget to mess around if you keep them interested.

Engagement can come from many different sources, and achieving this certainly doesn't mean that all your lessons have to be about fun and games. Your students also need to learn to slog away at a hard task, to develop self discipline, to be bored at times and still do as they're asked. But even the hardest lessons can be made engaging if you think creatively enough. You can also use the 'carrot' of a fun lesson in the future, to help your students get through the difficult ones.

As a professional educator, it's a matter of considering how your students learn best, and which approaches are most likely to get them behaving well. Students tend to learn and behave best when the teaching:

✓ Is multi sensory, with plenty of hands on activities and preferably something to see, touch, smell, hear and even taste;
✓ Feels relevant to the person who is being taught, for instance it's about a topic that person loves, or involves some kind of experience that is personal to the individual;
✓ Is active, interactive and fast paced;
✓ Seems full of variety, with plenty of different types of tasks that appeal to different kinds of learners;
✓ Incorporates different ways of learning, such as group work, research, paired discussions, hands on activities, explanations from the teacher.

Risky Teaching

As a teacher, it's your duty to constantly question and adapt the approaches you use. The day you say 'I know how to teach' is (to be frank) the day you should quit and go do something else. The best way to develop your own teaching is to try out new ideas, approaches, activities, on your class. Where you get the chance, you should also watch other teachers in action. If you're taking risks and trying out new things this can lead to some difficult behaviour. However, it will also teach you a great deal about classroom management. Plus, it's a lot more fun than always teaching from a text book or a worksheet.

If you're going to take risks and be more experimental, you've got to learn to trust your students. Some teachers will say that their students simply cannot be trusted. What this often means is that they tried something different one time, but the students couldn't handle it, and their behaviour was awful. However, you can't give up the first time you try, because your students need to get used to a different way of working. Equally, you cannot hope for someone to prove they deserve your trust, if you never give it to them in the first place.

When you try risky teaching:

✓ **Control it from the front:** Ask for a couple of volunteers to come up to the front and do the activity while the rest of the class watches. Use the chance to volunteer as a reward for good behaviour.
✓ **Keep it short:** It doesn't have to be the whole lesson – do a quick 'fun' activity between two longer less interesting ones.
✓ **Use the risky bit as the carrot:** Make it clear that, if behaviour falls apart, you will instantly stop the interesting activity and go back to the normal work.
✓ **Think about resources ahead of time:** Often, the reason risky activities go pear shaped is because something goes wrong with the way you've resourced them. Make sure there are enough resources for

everyone, and be clear with the students about how the resources must be used.

For some specific examples of 'risky teaching' activities, visit my website: www.suecowley.co.uk/lessons-i-love.html.

Let me finish by wishing the very best of luck with managing your students' behaviour, so that you can get on with the fun bit of teaching and inspiring them. With hard work and persistence, the Seven C's of Positive Behaviour Management will help you achieve this in your own classroom.

33280633R00033

Printed in Great Britain
by Amazon